TALKING, WRITING & THINKING ABOUT BOOKS

*101 ready-to-use
classroom activities that build
reading comprehension*

Jo Phenix

Pembroke Publishers Limited

Copyright © 2005 **Pembroke Publishers**
538 Hood Road
Markham, Ontario, Canada L3R 3K9
www.pembrokepublishers.com

Distributed in the U.S. by Stenhouse Publishers
477 Congress Street
Portland, ME 04101
www.stenhouse.com

All rights reserved.
No part of this publication may be reproduced in any form or by any means electronic or mechanical, including photocopy, recording, or any information, storage or retrieval system, without permission in writing from the publisher.

Every effort has been made to contact copyright holders for permission to reproduce borrowed material. The publishers apologize for any such omissions and will be pleased to rectify them in subsequent reprints of the book.

We acknowledge the financial support of the Government of Canada through the Book Publishing Industry Development Program (BPIDP) for our publishing activities.

We acknowledge the Government of Ontario through the Ontario Media Development Corporation's Ontario Book Initiative.

Library and Archives Canada Cataloguing in Publication

Phenix, Jo
   Talking, writing & thinking about books: 101 ready-to-use activities that build reading comprehension / Jo Phenix.

Includes index.
ISBN 1-55138-183-4

   1. Reading comprehension — Study and teaching (Elementary) — Activity programs. 2. Reading (Elementary) I. Title. II. Title: Talking, writing and thinking about books.

LB1573.7.P48 2005   372.47   C2004-907122-X

Editor: Kat Mototsune
Cover Design: John Zehethofer
Cover Photography: Photodisc
Typesetting: Jay Tee Graphics Ltd.

Printed and bound in Canada
9 8 7 6 5 4 3 2 1

Contents

Introduction   5

1 Talking and Reading Aloud   *11*

Character   *12*
Plot   *13*
Personal Response   *17*
Language and Words   *19*

2 Drama   *20*

Character   *21*
Plot   *31*

3 Visual Arts   *35*

Character   *36*
Setting   *44*
Plot   *49*

4 Writing   *61*

Character Description   *62*
Character and Events   *64*
Understanding Character   *67*
Setting   *76*
Plot Snapshot   *80*
Plot Retelling   *82*
Plot Summary   *88*
Personal Response/Opinions   *91*
Personal Response/New Ideas   *97*
Language and Words   *107*

5 Research   *113*

Author   *114*
Setting   *115*
Author/Setting/Genre   *116*

Appendix: Activity Assessment   *117*

Index of Activities   *121*

Introduction

Every activity in this book starts with reading.

Children read many different kinds of text in the classroom—novels, short stories, picture books, poems, scripts, magazines, newspaper articles. They experience media texts, such as films, videos, television, and advertisements. They may read individually, in a small group, in a guided-reading instructional situation, or with the whole class. The readings may be chosen and assigned by the teacher or self-selected by the child. Whatever a child's initial text experience, whether print or other media, the activities presented here are very adaptable. They can be used as part of many teaching situations, with a wide variety of texts, and with individuals, small groups, or the whole class.

The goal of the activities is to enhance comprehension.

We know that comprehension occurs when a reader relates what is being read or viewed to personal experience and prior knowledge. Comprehension is enhanced and strengthened—and demonstrated—when a reader is able to apply information from a text to new situations, either real or imaginary. For this deeper understanding to take place, children need to take a second or third look at their reading, to think about it from different points of view and with different emphases, and to inject their own opinions and ideas.

The activities in this book are designed primarily to engage students in thinking about their reading or viewing. (Do use them as a follow-up to viewing films and videos. The thinking process that leads to comprehension is the same.) As they complete the activities, students may be rereading parts of the text, skimming for specific information, rehearsing and presenting an oral reading, or reworking the text in a different format. They will be asked to go beyond the informational levels of reading, to reflect on what they have read, to analyze and interpret, to make judgments and comparisons. They will be asked to use their imaginations to hypothesize, predict, expand on the text, generate new ideas. They will approach the text from different points of view.

Working with the activities will help the students gain a deeper understanding of the text they have read. An even more important outcome is that they will be learning how to think like successful readers. They will learn that decoding words or giving an oral-reading performance is only part of the reading process; that a reader identifies with characters, wonders about motivations, senses mood, predicts possible outcomes, imagines settings and scenarios, develops tastes. This is the long-lasting learning they need to become fluent readers.

Because the activities are fun to do, encourage individual responses, allow wide flexibility in the method of responding, and often involve working with a partner or a group, they will help students develop a positive attitude towards reading. This will encourage them to become lifelong readers.

Each chapter focuses on a particular mode of response.

- Talking and Reading Aloud
- Drama
- Visual Arts
- Writing
- Research

The activities fall into five categories.

Each category establishes a primary focus, although you will find they frequently overlap one another. Not every category appears in each chapter. For example, language and words are less evident in visual arts activities, while exploring character is a prime focus in drama activities.

Character

Here the students will be able to project into and empathize with the experiences of the characters, recognizing different points of view, seeing relationships, and making inferences.

Setting

Thinking about setting helps children form sensory impressions, recall facts and details, place plot and characters in context, and appreciate descriptive language. They will activate their own prior knowledge and experience as they compare story settings with their own environment.

Plot

As they think about the plot, students will recall facts and details, place events in sequence, recognize cause and effect, hypothesize about possible actions and outcomes, make predictions and judgments, and solve problems. The activities ask students look at plot in three ways:

- A plot snapshot looks at one moment in time, one particular event or action in the book.
- Plot retelling focuses on the development of the story, the sequence of events, the motivations and outcomes.
- A plot summary focuses on the key points or events, the turning points of a story, the main ideas that move it forward.

You may find this terminology useful when you are discussing stories with students.

Personal Response

These activities encourage students to relate what they read to their own lives, environment, and experiences. As they talk, role-play, write, and think through the activities, they will be able to develop concepts, make connections, and validate and develop their own ideas, opinions, and values.

Language and Words

These activities ask students to look at specific words and their functions, such as descriptive language, strong verbs, or technical jargon. They will also take the children into the dictionary and thesaurus.

The activities will engage students through different groupings.

Although most activities are suitable for individual work, it is noted when they can be used for group work or work with a partner. For many activities this is flexible, and you can make your own decisions.

Whole-class interaction can occur as students display, present, and share their work.

Chapter	Kind of Activity	Reflection Focus	Individual Activity (page number)	Partner Activity (page number)	Group Activity (page number)
1	Talking and Reading Aloud	Character Plot Personal Response Language and Words	12 13–14 17 19	15	16 18
2	Drama	Character Plot	21–22	23–26	27–30 31–34
3	Visual Arts	Character Setting Plot	36–38 44–45 49–56	39–42 46 57–58	43 47–48 59–60

4	Writing	Character
		  Description
		  And Events
		  Understanding
		Setting
		Plot
		  Snapshot
		  Retelling
		  Summary
		Personal Response
		  Opinions
		  New Ideas
		Language and Words
			
			62–63
			64–65
			67–73
			76–77
			
			80–81
			82–85
			88–90
			
			91–96
			97–103
			107–110
				
				74–75
				
				104
				111
					
					66
					
					78–79
					
					86–87
					
					105–106
					112

5	Research	Author Setting Author, Setting, Genre	114 115		 116

How to use the activities

The activities are very versatile and will fulfill many of the requirements of a balanced literacy program. You will find many ways for them to fit naturally into your classroom organization. Here are a few suggestions.

Choosing Activities

- The activities are generic, and can be used after the reading of a wide variety of texts:

    Print texts—novels, short stories, poems, plays, newspapers, magazines
    Visual texts—picture books, cartoons
    Media texts—film, television, video

- There is no predetermined or recommended order in which to use the activities. You can make your choice according to the text a student is working with.
- You can use the Index of Activities on page 121 to choose specific modes of working that you want the students to experience—talking, visual arts, drama, writing, research.
- Students can choose from the activities on their own, or you can assign one that is suitable. Choosing an appropriate way to respond to a particular text will require further thinking and evaluation by the student. Making suitable choices is a learned skill; you may need to make the choices until students are familiar with this way of working and thinking.
- Students can use the same activity many times. Each activity will take on a new character when applied to a different text. Re-using an activity will also give students additional practice in particular modes of writing, talking, and working together.
- The activities are an ideal way for you to follow up on students' self-selected reading. Students can choose or you can assign an activity to accompany or follow the reading. These responses can form a starting point for a reading conference, as you talk to the students about their reading. When you cannot find time for a conference, many activities direct the student to talk and share with other students.

Groupings

- Some activities indicate working with a partner or a small group. These designations are suggestions only, and many activities are flexible enough for you to decide on the grouping. The chart on page 7 will help you decide what is best for each situation.
- Sometimes you may choose one activity for the whole class to work on as individuals. Students can then share and compare their responses in small groups, or in a plenary session of the whole class. An activity might become the preparation for a class discussion or debate: students do their own thinking and recording, then bring their ideas to the larger group.
- During a group novel study, you can select appropriate individual, partner, or group activities for different stages of the novel. Sharing ideas and responses throughout the reading of the novel can form the basis for literature circles.
- When the whole class has shared the same reading text or viewed the same video, you can assign different activities to small groups. Doing an activity the rest of the class has not done gives a real purpose for sharing and displaying.

Organizing the Activities

- The students can use the Activity Log on page 10 to keep their own record of activities they have completed.
- You may wish to provide each student with a ring binder or file folder in which to store the completed activities. This ongoing record will be useful to refer to when you are making a periodic assessment of a student's progress and achievement, or when talking with parents. The student's self-assessment pages and Activity Log may be filed here too.
- You can duplicate the pages on colored paper, color-coding them to correspond with each chapter: Talking and Reading Aloud, Visual Arts, Drama, Writing, Research. A quick look at the student's folder will indicate the range of modes a student is experiencing.
- In order to make self-selection of activities easier, you can mount each activity on colored card, laminate it, and store it in a box or file folder. Students can then browse through, make their selection, and take the card away to work with. In this case, it is a good idea to number the cards so they can be returned in the same order.
- If students are choosing their own activities, you can set some guidelines about how often they may repeat the same activity or choose from the same color-coded section.
- Students may need more space than the pages provide. They can use the back of the paper or a separate sheet to continue their writing.
- Many of the activities may be regarded as first-draft planning. You may choose not to develop these drafts, letting them serve as exploratory writing. There will be occasions for revising and editing by the students working alone or with help from you or a classmate. Students can then write a final draft for display or sharing.

Assessment

You can use the Assessment Master (page 118) in the Appendix to make a quick, general evaluation of a student's performance. When students first begin using the activities, you may wish to monitor all of them closely to assess their ability to work productively. Once you have a general idea of which students are working well and which need guidance from you, you can use the master more selectively. It is a good idea to tell students exactly what your assessment criteria are.

Activity Log

Name _____

Date	Activity	Comments

© 2005 *Talking, Writing and Thinking About Books* by Jo Phenix. Permission to copy for classroom use. Pembroke Publishers.

1 Talking and Reading Aloud

Oral reading has traditionally been a way for a teacher to assess the word accuracy of a child's reading. This is not the function of these activities. When students have had an opportunity to read with a specific purpose in mind, select a passage that is of particular interest or importance, and rehearse their presentation, oral reading can strengthen their understanding.

We know that talk plays an important role in helping children develop ideas and learn concepts; the quality and range of their thinking is enhanced through dialogue. When students generate ideas with a partner or in a group, the quality of their own writing improves. Talk activities also help children socialize.

These activities will engage students in exploratory and collaborative talk, as well as the more formal kinds of talk used in speeches and presentations.

Writing and Giving a Speech • Radio Advertisement • Show-and-Tell Talk • Songwriting and Singing • Book Talk • Oral Reading • Reading Emotions • Chalk Talk

Writing and Giving a Speech

Imagine one of the characters from the story has been invited to speak at your school. It is your job to write the speech.

1. List three things from the story the character might talk about.

_____   _____

_____

2. For each topic, write two or three sentences giving details.

Topic 1 _____

_____

_____

_____

Topic 2 _____

_____

_____

_____

Topic 3 _____

_____

_____

_____

3. Write a good opening sentence that will grab your listeners' attention.

_____

_____

4. Write a good ending to your speech.

_____

_____

5. Practise and give your speech in the role of the story character.

© 2005 *Talking, Writing and Thinking About Books* by Jo Phenix. Permission to copy for classroom use. Pembroke Publishers.

Radio Advertisement

Imagine the story is to be a radio play. Your job is to advertise the play on the radio.

1. Choose and practise a one-minute reading from the story to use in your ad.

2. Write an introduction.

3. Write a message for the end.

4. Record your commercial and leave it for others to listen to.

© 2005 *Talking, Writing and Thinking About Books* by Jo Phenix. Permission to copy for classroom use. Pembroke Publishers.

Show-and-Tell Talk

1. Think of an object that played an important part in the story.

Object: _____

2. Plan and rehearse a show-and-tell talk about this object.

Notes for Show-and-Tell

3. Either find the real object, or use a picture of the object.

4. Give your talk to a group of classmates.

© 2005 *Talking, Writing and Thinking About Books* by Jo Phenix. Permission to copy for classroom use. Pembroke Publishers.

Songwriting and Singing

Write a song about events in the story.

1. Choose a tune you know well.

   Title of Song: _____

2. Use the space here to write new words to go with the tune.

3. Practise singing your song.

4. Perform your song for another group.

Idea: You could teach your song to the other groups and form a choir.

© 2005 *Talking, Writing and Thinking About Books* by Jo Phenix. Permission to copy for classroom use. Pembroke Publishers.

Book Talk

Give a book talk to advertise the story.

1. Write a script for a five-minute talk.

2. Practise a five-minute reading from the story add to your talk.

3. Record or videotape your talk.

4. Put your recording where others can share it.

Idea: Will you add sound effects or music?

© 2005 *Talking, Writing and Thinking About Books* by Jo Phenix. Permission to copy for classroom use. Pembroke Publishers.

Oral Reading

1. Choose a passage from the story that is particularly exciting, sad, funny, scary, or descriptive (one that will take you about 5–10 minutes to read aloud).

   Story title _____

   Author _____

   Passage pages _____

2. Write the reasons why you chose this particular passage.

3. Rehearse an oral reading.
   - How will you add expression to your reading?
   - How will you make it interesting for your listeners?
   - Will you need to use different voices for the characters?
   - Would it be effective to play some background music?

4. Choose someone at school or at home to read your passage to.

5. After your reading, ask them to write how the passage made them feel.

© 2005 *Talking, Writing and Thinking About Books* by Jo Phenix. Permission to copy for classroom use. Pembroke Publishers.

Reading Emotions

1. Work together to list emotions you felt while reading the story.

2. Each person in the group choose one emotion and find a passage in the story that shows this emotion.

Emotions	Passages

3. Practise an oral reading of your passage.

4. Take turns reading your passages and discussing the emotions you felt.

Definition: An *emotion* is a feeling, such as anger, happiness, or jealousy.

© 2005 *Talking, Writing and Thinking About Books* by Jo Phenix. Permission to copy for classroom use. Pembroke Publishers.

Chalk Talk

Prepare a five-minute talk about the story.

1. Make a list of 5 words that are important to the story. The words could be names, places, clues, or feelings.

2. Plan to talk for one minute about why each word is important in the story.

Word	Importance
1. _____	
2. _____	
3. _____	
4. _____	
5. _____	

3. Print each word on the board or overhead projector as you give your talk.

4. Use your words to test the audience after your talk.

© 2005 *Talking, Writing and Thinking About Books* by Jo Phenix. Permission to copy for classroom use. Pembroke Publishers.

2 Drama

Drama allows children to enter into a story. Using drama, they can identify with a character, improvise, imagine, develop ideas, and solve problems.

The drama activities here provide a context for exploratory talk and group interaction. They will involve students in role-playing, mime, tableau, puppetry, and play-reading.

Speech in Character • News Script • Argument • Disagreement • Telephone Conversation • Gossip • Talk-Show Script • Awards Ceremony • Masks • Mime • Tableau • Paper-Bag Puppets • Play Reading • Puppet Show

Speech in Character

1. Imagine one of the characters is going to speak at your school assembly.

Character: _____

2. It will be your job to introduce the speaker. You will need to tell who the speaker is, a little about his or her life, and what he or she is going to talk about.

3. Write your speech.

4. Practise your speech.

5. Give your speech.

© 2005 *Talking, Writing and Thinking About Books* by Jo Phenix. Permission to copy for classroom use. Pembroke Publishers.

News Script

Imagine you are the scriptwriter for the TV news.

1. Write a two-minute story about one of the events in the story.

2. Practise reading your story aloud, to make sure it takes exactly two minutes.

3. Find an audience and perform your newscast for them.

© 2005 *Talking, Writing and Thinking About Books* by Jo Phenix. Permission to copy for classroom use. Pembroke Publishers.

Argument

1. Choose two characters in the story who might have an argument.

Character: _____

Character: _____

2. Take on the roles of the two characters.

3. Have your argument.

4. Switch parts and have your argument again. How is it different?

5. Afterwards, talk about the argument. Decide on the best way for the two characters to agree, and write it here.

© 2005 *Talking, Writing and Thinking About Books* by Jo Phenix. Permission to copy for classroom use. Pembroke Publishers.

Disagreement

1. Choose a child character from the story who got into trouble or who caused problems.

Character: _____

2. One person plays the child. The other person plays the child's parent.

3. Hold a conversation about the events in the story. Plan your talk so the two never agree about anything.

4. List the things you disagreed about. For each, think of a way to persuade the characters to agree.

Disagreement	Way to Agree

5. Switch parts and have your talk again. This time, let the two agree at the end.

© 2005 *Talking, Writing and Thinking About Books* by Jo Phenix. Permission to copy for classroom use. Pembroke Publishers.

Telephone Conversation

1. Imagine you are each a character from the story.

Character: _____   Character: _____

2. Hold a telephone conversation about events in the story.

3. Work together to write telephone messages for some of the other characters in the story.

4. Post your messages on a drawing of a refrigerator.

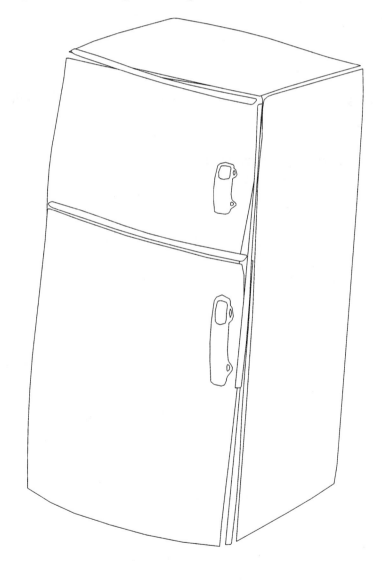

© 2005 *Talking, Writing and Thinking About Books* by Jo Phenix. Permission to copy for classroom use. Pembroke Publishers.

Gossip

1. Imagine you both are friends of one of the characters, and want to talk about the events in the story.

2. Decide where you are meeting.

   Place for Meeting: _____

   Why?

3. Rehearse a conversation you might have. Plan your conversation to be no more than five minutes.

4. Present your conversation to another group.

© 2005 *Talking, Writing and Thinking About Books* by Jo Phenix. Permission to copy for classroom use. Pembroke Publishers.

Talk-Show Script

1. Imagine you are the host of a TV talk-show. Some of the story characters are to be guests on your show.

Characters Who Will be Guests:

_____   _____

_____   _____

2. Work together to write a script for the show. Write parts for the host and all the guests.

3. Practise reading your script for the show with one person playing the host, the others playing the talk-show guests.

4. Find an audience and present your show. You can present your talk show live, or record it on videotape and then show it.

© 2005 *Talking, Writing and Thinking About Books* by Jo Phenix. Permission to copy for classroom use. Pembroke Publishers.

Awards Ceremony

1. Imagine some of the characters in the story are to receive awards. The awards will be for kind or brave deeds.

2. Make a list of the characters you could choose from. Choose one character for each person in the group.

3. Write a short speech about your assigned character, explaining what the award is being given for and why he or she deserves the award.

4. Hold the ceremony, make your speeches, and hand out your awards.

© 2005 *Talking, Writing and Thinking About Books* by Jo Phenix. Permission to copy for classroom use. Pembroke Publishers.

Masks

Make masks for characters or creatures in the story.

1. Choose one character for each person in the group.

2. Work together to design the masks.

   • How will you show what the character is like?

   • How will you show good or evil?

3. Now make your mask. Attach elastic or string to tie around your head.

4. Model your masks for another group. Explain who you are, and what part you play in the story.

© 2005 *Talking, Writing and Thinking About Books* by Jo Phenix. Permission to copy for classroom use. Pembroke Publishers.

Mime

1. Take turns choosing one character from the story. Do not tell the others who you are.

2. Mime a part of the story to show who your character is. What actions and facial expressions will you use?

3. Challenge the group to guess your character.

4. For each character, list the movements, expressions, or features that make it recognizable.

Character	Features

Definition: A *mime* is a play done without any sound. You use only actions and facial expressions.
Hint: If they guess quickly, you are doing a good mime.

© 2005 *Talking, Writing and Thinking About Books* by Jo Phenix. Permission to copy for classroom use. Pembroke Publishers.

Tableau

1. Choose 4 scenes from the story.
2. Use your bodies and simple objects to make a tableau for each scene.
3. Choose a title for each scene.
4. Invite another group to see your tableaux.

Story Title: _____ Author: _____

Scene 1 Title: _____

Scene 2 Title: _____

Scene 3 Title: _____

Scene 4 Title: _____

Scene 5 Title: _____

Definition: A *tableau* is a frozen picture, made with your bodies, in which nobody moves or speaks. Note: *Tableaux* is the plural of *tableau*, and is pronounced "ta-blow."

© 2005 *Talking, Writing and Thinking About Books* by Jo Phenix. Permission to copy for classroom use. Pembroke Publishers.

Paper-Bag Puppets

1. Choose a section of the story to present as a puppet play.

2. List the puppets you will need. Write notes on what they should look like.

Puppet	Appearance

3. Make paper-bag puppets.

   - Use brown paper bags
   - The bag will fit over your hand.
   - The bottom of the bag will be the top of the puppet's head.
   - Draw or paint the face on one side of the bag.

4. Practise and present your puppet play to another group.

> Hint: You can make your puppets more interesting by adding extras, like hair, a beard, earrings, a crown, glasses, a hat.

© 2005 *Talking, Writing and Thinking About Books* by Jo Phenix. Permission to copy for classroom use. Pembroke Publishers.

Play Reading

1. Choose a part of the story that is written in dialogue.

2. Read this section as a play. You will need one person for each character, and a narrator for the parts in between.

3. Switch parts and read again. Think — are there parts the narrator does not need to read aloud?

4. When you have rehearsed enough, find an audience and read your play.

Definition: *Dialogue* is when people are talking.
Hint: One person can read two smaller parts, using different voices.

© 2005 *Talking, Writing and Thinking About Books* by Jo Phenix. Permission to copy for classroom use. Pembroke Publishers.

Puppet Show

Design stick puppets and present your story as a puppet play.

1. Work by yourself to plan how each character will look.

2. Share and compare your designs with other group members. Make final decisions together on how each character will look.

3. Work together to make your puppets.

   - Decide on a size for the puppets so they match each other.
   - Draw each shape on stiff card and color it in.
   - Cut out each shape and fasten it to a stick with glue or tape.
   - Add extras like hair, hats, or clothing.

4. Use your puppets to tell the story. You may choose to present the whole story, or just one scene.

5. When you have practised enough, present your puppet play to another group.

© 2005 *Talking, Writing and Thinking About Books* by Jo Phenix. Permission to copy for classroom use. Pembroke Publishers.

3 Visual Arts

Activities such as drawing, painting, and modeling enable children to explore and express ideas without the constraints of written language. Visual arts activities may empower children to note specific details of character and setting. Telling a story through pictures can enable children to identify the key elements of a story and to represent them sequentially.

Activities include making board games, posters, murals, maps, scrapbooks, book covers, comic strips, and mobiles.

Greeting Card • Hat Design • Coat of Arms • *Wanted* Poster • Totem Pole • T-Shirt Design • Costume Design • Hall-of-Fame Portrait • Mapmaking • Room Design • Model Making • Landscape Painting • Mural • Timeline • Storyboard • Comic Strip • Overhead Script • CD Cover • Book Poster • Book Jacket • Book Cover • Scrapbook • Board Game • Animation • Mobile

Greeting Card

1. Imagine you are a greeting-card designer.

2. Design a card that might be used by one of the characters in the story.

   What event will it mark? _____

   Who will send it? _____

   Who will receive it? _____

3. Design your card here.

   Front of card   Back of card

4. Fold a piece of stiff paper and make your finished card.

   Inside

   Think: Will your message be a poem?

© 2005 *Talking, Writing and Thinking About Books* by Jo Phenix. Permission to copy for classroom use. Pembroke Publishers.

Hat Design

Imagine you are a hat designer. You have been asked to make hats for characters in the story.

1. List the characters you will make hats for.
2. Draw a picture of each hat.
3. Underneath each design, explain why this design is good for that person.

Character _____

Character _____

Character _____

Character _____

Think: Will any characters have words or signs on their hats?

© 2005 *Talking, Writing and Thinking About Books* by Jo Phenix. Permission to copy for classroom use. Pembroke Publishers.

Coat of Arms

Design a coat of arms for a character in the story.

1. Divide the shield shape into four parts.

2. In each part, draw and color an object that tells you something about the character.

3. Cut out and display your shield, along with the name of the character.

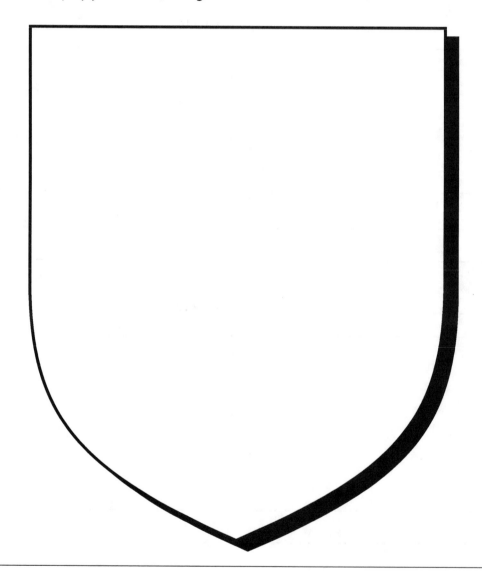

A *coat of arms* has pictures that tell something about the owner.

© 2005 *Talking, Writing and Thinking About Books* by Jo Phenix. Permission to copy for classroom use. Pembroke Publishers.

Wanted Poster

1. List the "bad guys" in the story. They might be people, animals, monsters, or any other creature
.

2. Together, design *Wanted* posters for 2 of the bad guys. Include

   • name, picture, and description
   • what the character is "wanted" for
   • where the character was last seen
   • any other important details

3. Choose one of your designs. Make a large poster to display on the bulletin board.

> *Wanted* posters are displayed in police stations to help catch criminals who are wanted by the law.

© 2005 *Talking, Writing and Thinking About Books* by Jo Phenix. Permission to copy for classroom use. Pembroke Publishers.

Totem Pole

Design a totem pole for a person or family in the story.

1. List between 4 and 6 objects that are important to the character or family of characters.

Character or Family: _____

Object: _____

Why it is important: _____

Object: _____

Why it is important: _____

Object: _____

Why it is important: _____

Object: _____

Why it is important: _____

Object: _____

Why it is important: _____

Object: _____

Why it is important: _____

2. Using play clay or modeling clay, model the objects.

3. Stack the objects to make the totem pole.

4. Display, and be ready to explain, your totem pole.

> The carvings on a totem pole show the history of a person or family.

© 2005 *Talking, Writing and Thinking About Books* by Jo Phenix. Permission to copy for classroom use. Pembroke Publishers.

T-Shirt Design

1. Choose 4 characters from the story.

2. List ideas for a T-shirt for each character.

   • Each shirt should show something special to that person.
   • Each shirt should have a message the person would like.

Character: _____   Character: _____

Picture: _____   Picture: _____

Message: _____   Message: _____

Character: _____   Character: _____

Picture: _____   Picture: _____

Message: _____   Message: _____

3. Choose one of your designs and draw the T-shirt.

4. Display your T-shirt designs, and be ready to explain them.

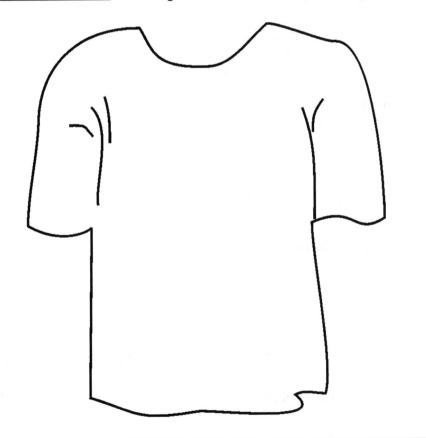

© 2005 *Talking, Writing and Thinking About Books* by Jo Phenix. Permission to copy for classroom use. Pembroke Publishers.

Costume Design

Imagine you are going to present the story as a play.

1. Design costumes for each of the characters.

Character: _____
Notes on Costume

Character: _____
Notes on Costume

Character: _____
Notes on Costume

Character: _____
Notes on Costume

Character: _____
Notes on Costume

2. On separate sheets of paper, draw, color, and label each design.

3. Set up a display of your costumes.

© 2005 *Talking, Writing and Thinking About Books* by Jo Phenix. Permission to copy for classroom use. Pembroke Publishers.

Hall-of-Fame Portrait

1. Together, choose characters from the story to put in a hall of fame. Talk about why you chose them. Each person in the group will be responsible for one "hall of famer."

2. Paint a portrait of your assigned character.

3. Draft a sign to display with your portrait. It should include the name of the character and why he or she is worthy of being in a hall of fame.

4. Work with a partner in the group to proofread and edit your writing.

5. Make an attractive final draft and display your hall of fame.

Definitions: A *hall of fame* recognizes people who have done something special. A *portrait* is a painting of a person.

© 2005 *Talking, Writing and Thinking About Books* by Jo Phenix. Permission to copy for classroom use. Pembroke Publishers.

Mapmaking

1. Plan a map showing the setting of your story. Be sure to include where events took place.

Places to Include on Map

2. Draw your map.

3. Label your map.

4. Use your map to tell a partner what happened in the story.

© 2005 *Talking, Writing and Thinking About Books* by Jo Phenix. Permission to copy for classroom use. Pembroke Publishers.

Room Design

Imagine you are going to design a room for a character or family in the story.

1. Make a list of important features the room will have.

2. Draw a floor plan that shows where the furniture will be.

3. Imagine you are standing in one spot in the room. On a separate sheet, draw or paint a picture of what you can see.

Idea: Perhaps you would like to make a model of the room and use it for storytelling.

© 2005 *Talking, Writing and Thinking About Books* by Jo Phenix. Permission to copy for classroom use. Pembroke Publishers.

Model Making

1. Plan a model of the setting of the story.

Items to Include in Model

2. Build your model using play clay, sand, cardboard, wood, fabric, or any other material you have.

3. Invite other classmates to view your model.

4. Use the model to give a talk about the story.

> Hint: You could use a pointer to highlight places on your model as you give your talk.

© 2005 *Talking, Writing and Thinking About Books* by Jo Phenix. Permission to copy for classroom use. Pembroke Publishers.

Landscape Painting

1. Work together to choose several different places in the story. Talk about what each one looks like and make a list of what will be in each picture.

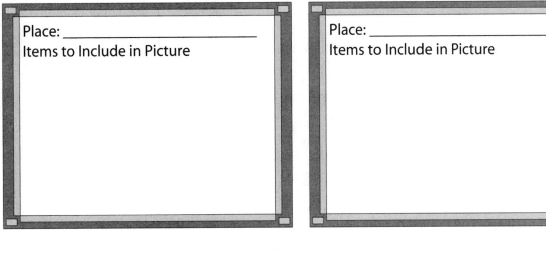

Place: _____
Items to Include in Picture

Place: _____
Items to Include in Picture

Place: _____
Items to Include in Picture

Place: _____
Items to Include in Picture

2. Each person paint a landscape of one of the places. Add a title to your landscape.

3. Set up a display of your landscapes.

Definition: A *landscape* is a picture of a place, rather than of a person.

© 2005 *Talking, Writing and Thinking About Books* by Jo Phenix. Permission to copy for classroom use. Pembroke Publishers.

Mural

1. Plan a mural showing events and places in the story.

Events and Places for Mural

Design for Mural

2. Work together to paint the mural.

3. Display your mural

4. Find a small audience and use your mural for storytelling.

> Definition: A *mural* is a large painting showing many different scenes. It is usually painted or displayed on a wall.

© 2005 *Talking, Writing and Thinking About Books* by Jo Phenix. Permission to copy for classroom use. Pembroke Publishers.

Timeline

Make a timeline showing the events of the story.

1. Choose an interesting way to present your timeline. It should show movement along some kind of track or line. It could be a

- staircase
- road
- river

- train on a track
- downhill skier

2. List events from the story on your timeline.

3. Create your timeline

4. Use your timeline for storytelling.

Think: What kind of line will you choose?

© 2005 *Talking, Writing and Thinking About Books* by Jo Phenix. Permission to copy for classroom use. Pembroke Publishers.

Storyboard

Imagine you are going to make a film of the story. Make a storyboard for the film.

1. Make up a title for your film. It does not have to be the same as the book title.

Title: _____

2. Choose 6 scenes you will need. For each one, draw a picture of the scene, and write the main events that will take place in that scene.

Definition: The maker of a movie or video uses a *storyboard* to show what will be happening on the screen.

© 2005 *Talking, Writing and Thinking About Books* by Jo Phenix. Permission to copy for classroom use. Pembroke Publishers.

Comic Strip

Retell the story in a comic strip.

1. Choose 8 scenes to tell the story.

	Picture	Speech
Scene 1		
Scene 2		
Scene 3		
Scene 4		
Scene 5		
Scene 6		
Scene 7		
Scene 8		

1. Fold a piece of paper into 8 sections

2. Draw one picture in each section.

3. Add speech balloons and/or a sentence at the bottom of each picture to tell the story.

Think: Who will you share your comic strip with?

© 2005 *Talking, Writing and Thinking About Books* by Jo Phenix. Permission to copy for classroom use. Pembroke Publishers.

Overhead Script

1. Plan a series of pictures to tell the story.

2. Write a script of two or three sentences for each picture.

3. Using overhead transparencies and erasable markers, draw your pictures.

4. Practise reading your script as you show the pictures. How will you make your reading entertaining?

5. Present your retelling to another group.

Hint: You may want to try out your pictures on paper first.

© 2005 *Talking, Writing and Thinking About Books* by Jo Phenix. Permission to copy for classroom use. Pembroke Publishers.

CD Cover

Imagine you have made a CD recording of the story.

1. Design a cover for the CD case.

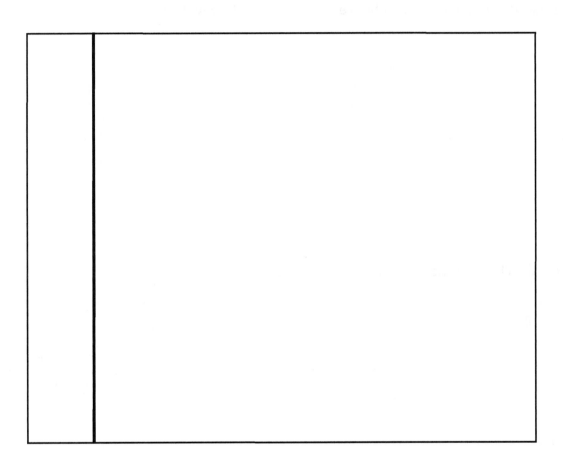

2. Write brief notes about the story for the back of the case.

3. Use an empty CD case to display your new CD cover.

© 2005 *Talking, Writing and Thinking About Books* by Jo Phenix. Permission to copy for classroom use. Pembroke Publishers.

Book Poster

1. Imagine you own a bookstore.

   Name your bookstore _____

2. List 5 things you would tell people to encourage them to buy the book.

3. Make a sketch of a scene from the book that would help to sell it.

4. Use your picture and information from your list to make a poster advertising the book. Proofread your work carefully before you make the final draft.

5. Display your poster.

> Hint: People must be able to read a poster from a distance.

© 2005 *Talking, Writing and Thinking About Books* by Jo Phenix. Permission to copy for classroom use. Pembroke Publishers.

Book Jacket

1. Write a blurb of between 30 and 40 words for the story.

2. Design a jacket for the book. Include a new picture for the front of the jacket.

3. Fold paper to make the jacket for the book.

4. Put your new design on the front.

5. Print your blurb on the back.

> Definition: A *blurb* is a short account of the story that appears on the back cover of a book.

© 2005 *Talking, Writing and Thinking About Books* by Jo Phenix. Permission to copy for classroom use. Pembroke Publishers.

Book Cover

Design a new cover for your book.

1. Choose an interesting part of the story.

2. Plan a picture for the cover.

3. Choose an interesting letter style for the title.

4. Make your final draft: draw the picture and print the name of the author and illustrator on the cover.

5. Display your new cover.

© 2005 *Talking, Writing and Thinking About Books* by Jo Phenix. Permission to copy for classroom use. Pembroke Publishers.

Scrapbook

1. Choose a character from the story.

Character: _____

2. Make a list of items and pictures that person might put into a scrapbook to remind them of events in the story.

3. Make, write, or draw the items for the scrapbook.

4. Fold several pieces of paper to make the scrapbook. Paste in your items.

5. Make a cover that includes the character's name.

Definition: A *scrapbook* is a collection of photographs, newspaper clippings, cards, etc. Each piece has a special meaning for the owner.

© 2005 *Talking, Writing and Thinking About Books* by Jo Phenix. Permission to copy for classroom use. Pembroke Publishers.

Board Game

Design a board game based on the story.

1. Use the setting to design a game board.

2. Use events in the story to bring good luck or bad luck.

Events in the Story

Good Luck	Bad Luck

3. Write the rules of the game.

4. Make your game board.

5. Teach another group how to play.

© 2005 *Talking, Writing and Thinking About Books* by Jo Phenix. Permission to copy for classroom use. Pembroke Publishers.

Animation

Imagine you are a team working for Disney. You are going to make some designs for an animated movie of the story.

1. Plan your animated characters.

Character: _____   Character: _____

Character: _____   Character: _____

1. Draw or paint each of the characters.

2. Draw a series of background pictures showing places in the movie.

3. Label your designs and mount them for a display.

© 2005 *Talking, Writing and Thinking About Books* by Jo Phenix. Permission to copy for classroom use. Pembroke Publishers.

Mobile

Create a mobile based on the story.

1. List 8 to 10 objects that are important in the story. Describe each object.

2. Make a model or cut-out of each one. Use cardboard, wood, play clay, plastic foam, or any other material you have.

3. Hang your objects from a wire coat hanger.

4. Hang the title of the story and the author's name somewhere in your mobile.

5. Find a place to hang your mobile.

Definition: A *mobile* is made by hanging objects or pictures from a holder.

© 2005 *Talking, Writing and Thinking About Books* by Jo Phenix. Permission to copy for classroom use. Pembroke Publishers.

4 Writing

We know that writing is more than a way to show what we know—it is a way of thinking and learning.

As well as guiding students to take a second look at many aspects of their reading, the activities will give them opportunities to use different modes of writing—informational, personal, and poetic—and to write for different purposes and audiences. From "adding to the story" to "your diary," the activities provide opportunities for both instruction and practice.

Most of these activities are exploratory in nature, and give students opportunities to try out ideas in a low-risk situation. Make sure they are aware that there are no right or wrong answers, and that, while their responses should have reference to the story they have read, they are encouraged to be creative and use their imagination.

The responses will be first-draft writing, so students should feel free to change their minds and cross out without paying undue attention to neatness and spelling. In some activities you may choose to have students revise and edit these drafts, to work towards a final draft with correct spelling and good presentation. It is a good idea for students to produce a final draft only when the writing is to be shared, published, or displayed.

Character Description • Word-List Poem • E-Mail Friend • Sticky Notes • Character Diary • Friendly Letter • Job Interview • School Report • Gift List • Adding to the Story • Giving Advice • Job Letter • *Who Am I?* Quiz • Web Site • Setting Description • *House for Sale* Advertisement • Picture Postcards • Travel Brochure • Newspaper Editorial • Memoir • Newspaper Headlines • Biography • Quiz Questions • Story Staircase • Reunion Conversation • Newspaper Front Page • Story Summary • Movie Title • TV Guide • Comparing and Contrasting • List of Rules • Alien Report • Bumper Sticker • Book Review • Fact or Fantasy • Table of Contents • Sequel • Problem Solving • Rules Poster • New Character • Author Letter • Your Diary • Party Plan • Time Capsule • Adoption Posters • Descriptive Language • Dictionary • Glossary • Thesaurus • Word Collage • Alphabet Book

Character Description

Imagine you are going to present the story as a play.

1. You need to choose actors to play each part.
2. List the names of the main characters who would be in the play.
3. For each one, write a 20-word description. Include age, appearance, and behavior.

Character: _____

_____

_____

_____

Character: _____

_____

_____

_____

Character: _____

_____

_____

_____

Character: _____

_____

_____

_____

Character: _____

_____

_____

_____

© 2005 *Talking, Writing and Thinking About Books* by Jo Phenix. Permission to copy for classroom use. Pembroke Publishers.

Word-List Poem

Here is an example of a word-list poem with 7 lines:

Miserable
Young
Overworked
Lucky
Magical
Happy
Cinderella.

Write your own word-list poem.

1. Choose a character from the story.

2. List 6 adjectives describing the character.

3. For the final line, add the character's name.

_____

_____

_____

_____

_____

_____

_____

Hint: Did you notice that Cinderella's adjectives started out sad and became happy, just like her life in the story? Can you show a change of mood in your poem?

© 2005 *Talking, Writing and Thinking About Books* by Jo Phenix. Permission to copy for classroom use. Pembroke Publishers.

E-Mail Friend

Imagine you could have a character from the story as an e-mail pal.

1. Think about who you would choose.

Character : _____

2. Create an e-mail address for your pal.

E-mail address: _____

3. Write a series of e-mails between you and pal. Base them on what happens in the story.

> Think: What can you find out about the story from your new e-mail pal?

© 2005 *Talking, Writing and Thinking About Books* by Jo Phenix. Permission to copy for classroom use. Pembroke Publishers.

Sticky Notes

1. Choose 3 characters from the story.

_____   _____   _____

2. Write a sticky note each character might have written at some time in the story. Show who each note is written for.

3. Think about where each sticky note might have been stuck.

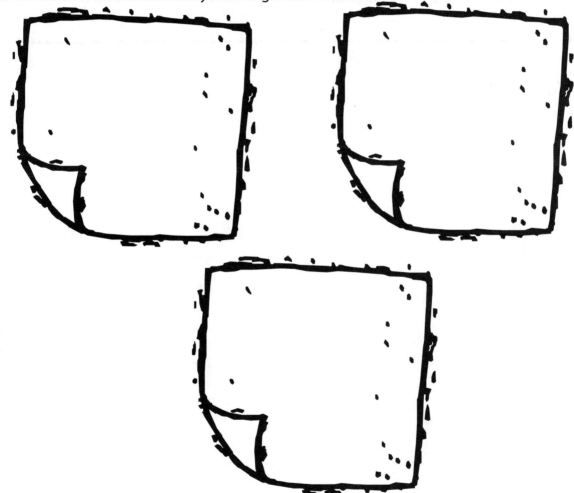

Definition: *Sticky notes* stick to any surface, and are removable. You use them to send messages and reminders.

© 2005 *Talking, Writing and Thinking About Books* by Jo Phenix. Permission to copy for classroom use. Pembroke Publishers.

Character Diary

1. Imagine each of you is a character in the story.

2. Choose an event in the story in which you all appeared.

3. As the character, write your diary entry for that day.

4. Take turns to read your diary entries aloud.

5. Talk about how your accounts were the same or different.

Dear Diary

© 2005 *Talking, Writing and Thinking About Books* by Jo Phenix. Permission to copy for classroom use. Pembroke Publishers.

Friendly Letter

1. Imagine you are one of the characters in the story. In the first letter form, write a letter to a friend asking for advice.

2. In the second letter form, write the friend's answering letter.

Dear _____

Dear _____

Hint: Will the friend be sympathetic or critical?

© 2005 *Talking, Writing and Thinking About Books* by Jo Phenix. Permission to copy for classroom use. Pembroke Publishers.

Job Interview

Imagine one of the characters in the story has applied for a job to teach at your school. You are on the interviewing team.

1. Choose the character you think would make the most interesting teacher.

Character: _____

2. Write 3 questions you would ask at the interview.

3. Write the answers you might get.

4. Work with a classmate to read aloud your question and answers.

Interview Notes for Teaching Position

1. Q: _____

   A: _____

     _____

2. Q: _____

   A: _____

     _____

3. Q: _____

   A: _____

     _____

> Think: When reading aloud, will you be yourself or the character?

© 2005 *Talking, Writing and Thinking About Books* by Jo Phenix. Permission to copy for classroom use. Pembroke Publishers.

School Report

Imagine you are writing a school report on two of the characters.

1. Choose one "good" character and one "not-so-good" character.
2. Report on each character's behavior, achievements, and failings.

SCHOOL REPORT		
Character's Name _____		
Report submitted to _____		
Subject	**Mark**	**Comments**
Suggestions for future work and behavior		

SCHOOL REPORT		
Character's Name _____		
Report submitted to _____		
Subject	**Mark**	**Comments**
Suggestions for future work and behavior		

© 2005 *Talking, Writing and Thinking About Books* by Jo Phenix. Permission to copy for classroom use. Pembroke Publishers.

Gift List

Imagine you are giving a birthday gift to each of the main characters in the story.

1. Think of a gift you think each one would like to receive.

2. Make a list of the gifts. Beside each one, write why you think it is just right.

Character	Gift	Why

3. On a separate sheet, draw a picture of each gift. Add a gift tag to say who it is for.

© 2005 *Talking, Writing and Thinking About Books* by Jo Phenix. Permission to copy for classroom use. Pembroke Publishers.

Adding to the Story

Imagine you can make a wish come true for some of the characters in the story.

1. Choose 3 characters. For each one, write what their wish might be.

Character: _____

Wish: _____

Character: _____

Wish: _____

Character: _____

Wish: _____

2. Choose one of the wishes. Write a story about what might happen if the wish was granted.

3. Share your story with someone at school or at home.

© 2005 *Talking, Writing and Thinking About Books* by Jo Phenix. Permission to copy for classroom use. Pembroke Publishers.

Giving Advice

1. Choose 3 characters from the story.
2. For each character, write three "dos" and three "don'ts" that you think would help them in the future.

Character: _____

Dos   Don'ts

1.   1.

2.   2.

3.   3.

Character: _____

Dos   Don'ts

1.   1.

2.   2.

3.   3.

Character: _____

Dos   Don'ts

1.   1.

2.   2.

3.   3.

3. Choose one of the characters. Write what his or her reaction might be to your advice.

© 2005 *Talking, Writing and Thinking About Books* by Jo Phenix. Permission to copy for classroom use. Pembroke Publishers.

Job Letter

Imagine you are one of the characters in the story, and you are applying for a job.

1. Write a letter to the employer.

   - Explain which job you are applying for.
   - Explain why you want the job.
   - Explain why you think you are suited for the job

2. Ask a partner who knows the story to reply to your letter.

Dear _____	Dear _____

Hint: Will your partner agree that you are right for the job, or not?

© 2005 *Talking, Writing and Thinking About Books* by Jo Phenix. Permission to copy for classroom use. Pembroke Publishers.

Who Am I? Quiz

1. Working separately, each choose 2 or 3 characters from the story.

2. Write three clues about each person.

Character: _____

Clues: 1. _____

2. _____

3. _____

Character: _____

Clues: 1. _____

2. _____

3. _____

Character: _____

Clues: 1. _____

2. _____

3. _____

3. Hold a *Who am I?* quiz.

- Read aloud your clues one at a time.
- Challenge your partner to guess the character.

4. Print all the questions on a card. Print the answers on the back.

5. Leave your quiz card in the book for the next reader to try.

© 2005 *Talking, Writing and Thinking About Books* by Jo Phenix. Permission to copy for classroom use. Pembroke Publishers.

Web Site

Imagine you are a web designer. Design a web site for one of the characters from the story.

1. List 5 different things the character is interested in, or is good at.

1. _____   2. _____

3. _____   4. _____

5. _____

2. Use these ideas to make a home page.

3. Design a page for each of these 5 items, with information and pictures.
Notes for Pages

4. Create an address for the site: www. _____

5. Invite other classmates to visit your site. Record the number of "hits" you get.

© 2005 *Talking, Writing and Thinking About Books* by Jo Phenix. Permission to copy for classroom use. Pembroke Publishers.

Setting Description

1. Think about where the story is set.

2. Write a paragraph describing how the setting is similar to where you live.

3. Write a paragraph describing how it is unlike where you live.

4. Finish with a paragraph explaining which place you would prefer to live, and why.

Where I Would Prefer to Live: _____
Why

© 2005 *Talking, Writing and Thinking About Books* by Jo Phenix. Permission to copy for classroom use. Pembroke Publishers.

House for Sale Advertisement

Imagine you live where this story took place, but you want to move away. Write a newspaper advertisement to sell your house.

1. Draw a picture of your house.

2. Write a description of the area that would help to sell your house.

- What are the places of interest?
- What features would make it a good place to live?
- Which people would make good neighbors?

3. Display your advertisement.

© 2005 *Talking, Writing and Thinking About Books* by Jo Phenix. Permission to copy for classroom use. Pembroke Publishers.

Picture Postcards

1. Each person choose one character from the story. Each character is sending a postcard from a place in the story to a friend.
2. Draw a picture of the place on the front of the card.
3. On the left side of the back, write a message about the place pictured and what happened there.
4. Write the friend's name and address on the right side.

Front

Back

5. Exchange cards, and write an answer.

© 2005 *Talking, Writing and Thinking About Books* by Jo Phenix. Permission to copy for classroom use. Pembroke Publishers.

Travel Brochure

Imagine you work for a travel agency. Your job today is to write a brochure for the place where the story is set.

1. Each person choose a different topic from the story.

2. For your topic:

   - Draw a picture
   - Write a description to make the setting sound attractive
   - Write reasons why people should visit

3. Work together to edit your brochure.

4. Publish and display your finished brochure.

© 2005 *Talking, Writing and Thinking About Books* by Jo Phenix. Permission to copy for classroom use. Pembroke Publishers.

Newspaper Editorial

Write an editorial for your local newspaper about an event in the story.

1. Write paragraph 1: Explain what happened and how people behaved.

2. Write paragraph 2: Write your thoughts and opinions about the event. For example:

   • Did the characters do the right thing?
   • How do you feel about how they behaved?

3. Write paragraph 3: Write your suggestions for the characters.

Definition: An *editorial* is a piece of writing in which you give your opinion.
Hint: A good editorial makes it clear how you think and feel about what happened.

© 2005 *Talking, Writing and Thinking About Books* by Jo Phenix. Permission to copy for classroom use. Pembroke Publishers.

Memoir

1. Imagine you are one of the characters in the story, now an old person.

2. Choose one of the events in the story. Write a chapter about this event for your memoir.

- Paragraph 1: Retell the event as you remember it.

- Paragraph 2: Tell how you felt about the event and the other people at the time.

- Paragraph 3: Write about how you feel about it now that you are old.

- Paragraph 4: If you could live the event over again, would you act in the same way? What might be different?

Definition: A *memoir* is a personal, written memory of past events in your life.
Think: If you could live the event again, would you act in the same way?

© 2005 *Talking, Writing and Thinking About Books* by Jo Phenix. Permission to copy for classroom use. Pembroke Publishers.

Newspaper Headlines

Imagine you are the headline writer for a newspaper.

1. Choose 6 events in the story that would make good newspaper stories.

2. Come up with an effective headline for each of these stories.

Event: _____

Headline: _____

Event: _____

Headline: _____

Event: _____

Headline: _____

Event:_____

Headline: _____

Event:_____

Headline _____:

Event:_____

Headline: _____

3. Print your headlines in different sizes.

4. Paste up your front page, using your headlines.

Definitions: Newspaper *headlines* are titles for stories. They have to be quite short, and they have to catch the reader's attention. *Pasting up* is arranging the placement of stories on a newspaper page.
Hint: The headline for the main story should go at the top and be in the biggest print.

© 2005 *Talking, Writing and Thinking About Books* by Jo Phenix. Permission to copy for classroom use. Pembroke Publishers.

Biography

1. Choose one of the characters from the story.

Character: _____

2. Write 6 to 10 chapter titles that might appear in that person's biography. The chapter titles should give an idea of the main events of the story.

Chapter 1: _____

Chapter 2: _____

Chapter 3: _____

Chapter 4: _____

Chapter 5: _____

Chapter 6: _____

Chapter 7: _____

Chapter 8: _____

Chapter 9: _____

Chapter 10: _____

3. Share and discuss your chapter titles with someone who has read the story.

Definition: A *biography* is a person's life story.

© 2005 *Talking, Writing and Thinking About Books* by Jo Phenix. Permission to copy for classroom use. Pembroke Publishers.

Quiz Questions

1. Make up 10 quiz questions based on the story.

Q: _____

A: _____

Q: _____

A: _____

Q: _____

A: _____

Q: _____

A: _____

Q: _____

A: _____

Q: _____

A: _____

Q: _____

A: _____

Q: _____

A: _____

Q: _____

A: _____

Q: _____

A: _____

2. Write the questions on one sheet of paper, and the answers on another.
3. Find someone else who has read the story. Have them take the quiz.
4. Check the answers, and give a score out of 10.
5. Leave the questions in the book for the next reader to try. Leave your name, so you can check the next reader's answers.

© 2005 *Talking, Writing and Thinking About Books* by Jo Phenix. Permission to copy for classroom use. Pembroke Publishers.

Story Staircase

Think of traveling through your story as like climbing stairs.

1. Make a list of the most important events of the story.

2. Draw a staircase and print an event on each step. Your list of events should start on the bottom step and end on the top step.

3. Fill in a background for your staircase that fits the story.

© 2005 *Talking, Writing and Thinking About Books* by Jo Phenix. Permission to copy for classroom use. Pembroke Publishers.

Reunion Conversation

Imagine you are characters from the story meeting again after 20 years.

1. Each person choose one character to role-play.

2. As the characters, hold the conversation you might have at your reunion.
   • What will you remember?
   • What will you talk about?
   • Will you be friendly or argue?

3. Switch parts and hold the conversation again.

4. Work together to write a letter to a character not at the reunion. Tell them how the meeting went, and what you all talked about

© 2005 *Talking, Writing and Thinking About Books* by Jo Phenix. Permission to copy for classroom use. Pembroke Publishers.

Newspaper Front Page

Prepare the front page of a newspaper.

1. Work together to make a list of important events from the story.

2. Each person choose one event from the list.

3. For your own event, write a headline and the story. Add a picture.

4. Work together to revise and edit your stories.

5. Make your own final draft.

6. Paste up your stories to make the full front page.

7. Add a title for the newspaper.

   Newspaper Title: _____

8. Put your finished newspaper where others can read it.

Definitions: Newspaper *headlines* are titles for stories. They have to be quite short, and they have to catch the reader's attention. *Pasting up* is arranging the placement of stories on a newspaper page.

© 2005 *Talking, Writing and Thinking About Books* by Jo Phenix. Permission to copy for classroom use. Pembroke Publishers.

Story Summary

Write a summary of the story.

1. List the names of the main characters in the story.

2. List the important events.

3. List any feelings, opinions, or ideas that were important to the story.

4. In a summary of 30 to 40 words, retell the story, including the most important facts from your list.

5. Use your summary to give a book talk to a small group.

6. Leave your summary in the book for the next reader to find.

Definition: A *summary* tells the most important parts of the story in a very few words.

© 2005 *Talking, Writing and Thinking About Books* by Jo Phenix. Permission to copy for classroom use. Pembroke Publishers.

Movie Title

Imagine you are a movie producer. You are going to make a movie of the story.

1. Write 4 possible titles that are different from the book title.

Book Title: _____

Movie Title 1: _____

Movie Title 2: _____

Movie Title 3: _____

Movie Title 4: _____

2. Circle the one that you would choose.

3. Compose an e-mail to the author, explaining why your title is a better choice for the movie.

4. Write the author's possible reply.

© 2005 *Talking, Writing and Thinking About Books* by Jo Phenix. Permission to copy for classroom use. Pembroke Publishers.

TV Guide

Imagine you are going to make the story into a four-part TV series.

1. Decide how you would divide the story into 4 parts.

2. Write a title for each part.

3. For each part, write a 20-word description for the TV guide. Include what will happen in that episode.

Series Title: _____

Part 1 Title: _____

Part 2 Title: _____

Part 3 Title: _____

Part 4 Title: _____

© 2005 *Talking, Writing and Thinking About Books* by Jo Phenix. Permission to copy for classroom use. Pembroke Publishers.

Comparing and Contrasting

1. Think of another story you have read that is similar to this one. It might be

   - by the same author
   - about the same kind of events or people
   - set in the same kind of place

Names of the two stories:

Title: _____

                    Author: _____

Title: _____

                    Author: _____

2. Write 3 ways in which the stories are similar.

   1. _____
   2. _____
   3. _____

3. Write 3 ways in which they are different.

   1. _____
   2. _____
   3. _____

4. Which one did you like best? _____

   Explain why.

© 2005 *Talking, Writing and Thinking About Books* by Jo Phenix. Permission to copy for classroom use. Pembroke Publishers.

List of Rules

1. Think about how the story presented ideas of what is right and wrong.

2. List 3 actions in the story that you think were wrong.

    1.

    2.

    3.

3. List 3 actions you think were right.

    1.

    2.

    3.

4. Write 3 tests of your own to help people tell right from wrong.

    1.

    2.

    3.

5. Make a poster to display your 3 tests.

© 2005 *Talking, Writing and Thinking About Books* by Jo Phenix. Permission to copy for classroom use. Pembroke Publishers.

Alien Report

Imagine you are a visitor from a distant planet. You have landed on Earth in the middle of the story.

1. Write a report to your home planet.

   - What do you see happening?
   - What seems strange to you?
   - How do you explain what you see?

2. Decide who you will send your report to. Address an envelope, and put your report inside.

© 2005 *Talking, Writing and Thinking About Books* by Jo Phenix. Permission to copy for classroom use. Pembroke Publishers.

Bumper Sticker

1. Make a list of 5 lessons someone might learn from the story.

   1.

   2.

   3.

   4.

   5.

2. Write a bumper sticker or banner message of no more than 10 words for each lesson. How will you make your bumper stickers eye-catching and attractive?

3. Display your bumper stickers.

   Definition: Designed to be displayed on car bumpers, *bumper stickers* are usually short lessons or statements to attract attention and make people think.

© 2005 *Talking, Writing and Thinking About Books* by Jo Phenix. Permission to copy for classroom use. Pembroke Publishers.

Book Review

1. Write a review of your story in 40 to 50 words. Your review should include these things:

   - what the story was about
   - what you liked or disliked about it
   - whether you would recommend it to others
   - who would most enjoy it

2. Display your review where others can read it.

Definition: A *review* gives one person's opinion about a book, movie, play, etc.

© 2005 *Talking, Writing and Thinking About Books* by Jo Phenix. Permission to copy for classroom use. Pembroke Publishers.

Fact or Fantasy

Could the events in the story have really happened?

List 3 events from the story that could happen in real life.

1. _____

I chose this event because _____

_____

2. _____

I chose this event because _____

_____

3. _____

I chose this event because _____

_____

List 3 events from the story that would be unlikely to happen in real life.

1. _____

I chose this event because _____

_____

2. _____

I chose this event because _____

_____

3. _____

I chose this event because _____

_____

© 2005 *Talking, Writing and Thinking About Books* by Jo Phenix. Permission to copy for classroom use. Pembroke Publishers.

Table of Contents

Imagine you are writing a new book about the same characters as in the story.

1. Jot down some brief notes about what will happen in the story.

2. Write the table of contents for your new book. Use 6 to 10 chapter headings. Each chapter should tell one part of the story.

Chapter 1: _____

Chapter 2: _____

Chapter 3: _____

Chapter 4: _____

Chapter 5: _____

Chapter 6: _____

Chapter 7: _____

Chapter 8: _____

Chapter 9: _____

Chapter 10: _____

Idea: Perhaps you would like to complete this story.

© 2005 *Talking, Writing and Thinking About Books* by Jo Phenix. Permission to copy for classroom use. Pembroke Publishers.

Sequel

1. At the end of the story, think about what might happen next.

2. Write a possible next chapter.

3. Share your sequel with someone who has read the same story.

4. Discuss your ideas.

Definition: A *sequel* is a follow-up story that continues where the original story finished.

© 2005 *Talking, Writing and Thinking About Books* by Jo Phenix. Permission to copy for classroom use. Pembroke Publishers.

Problem Solving

1. List 3 problems that characters in the story had to solve.

2. Beside each one, write how it was solved.

3. For each problem, write a different solution that could have been tried.

Problem #1	Story Solution	My Solution

Problem #2	Story Solution	My Solution

Problem #3	Story Solution	My Solution

4. Ask a friend to judge which solutions are the best.

© 2005 *Talking, Writing and Thinking About Books* by Jo Phenix. Permission to copy for classroom use. Pembroke Publishers.

Rules Poster

1. List 3 bad things that happened in the story.

2. For each one, explain why it happened.

3. For each one, write a new rule or law that would prevent the bad thing happening again.

Bad Thing 1   Why It Happened

_____   _____

New Rule:

Bad Thing 2   Why It Happened

_____   _____

New Rule:

Bad Thing 3   Why It Happened

_____   _____

New Rule:

4. Make a poster to let people know the new rules.

© 2005 *Talking, Writing and Thinking About Books* by Jo Phenix. Permission to copy for classroom use. Pembroke Publishers.

New Character

Imagine you could add an extra character to the story.

1. Think about who the new character would be.

New Character: _____

2. Write a description of your character: name, appearance, behavior, likes and dislikes, etc.

3. Explain how the story would be changed with your new character in it.

© 2005 *Talking, Writing and Thinking About Books* by Jo Phenix. Permission to copy for classroom use. Pembroke Publishers.

Author Letter

Write a letter to the author of the story.

1. Write a first draft:

Dear _____

Paragraph 1: Write your comments on the story.

Paragraph 2: Ask a question or two, and explain why you want to know the answer.

End your letter.

3. Work with a partner to revise and edit your draft.

4. Write your final draft.

5. Mail your letter to the author at the publisher's address in the book.

© 2005 *Talking, Writing and Thinking About Books* by Jo Phenix. Permission to copy for classroom use. Pembroke Publishers.

Your Diary

1. Choose an interesting or exciting part of the story that you would like to have been involved in.

2. Imagine yourself in this part of the story. Who will you be? What will you do?

3. Write your diary entry, describing the experience.

Think: Who will you share your diary entry with?

© 2005 *Talking, Writing and Thinking About Books* by Jo Phenix. Permission to copy for classroom use. Pembroke Publishers.

Party Plan

1. Think of an event in the story that could be a reason to hold a party.

Event: _____

2. Make a list of people from the story who would be invited.

3. Write a party invitation. Include

- what the party is for
- when and where it is
- what to wear
- what to bring

3. Imagine you are newspaper reporters at the party. Write a 50-word report on the party for your paper. Include

- who was there
- what the decorations looked like
- what happened at the party

4. Add a picture and headline to your story.

Idea: Will the party have a theme?

© 2005 *Talking, Writing and Thinking About Books* by Jo Phenix. Permission to copy for classroom use. Pembroke Publishers.

Time Capsule

1. List objects that characters in the story might put in a time capsule. Add their reasons for choosing those objects.

Object	Chosen by	Reasons for choosing

2. Decide where you will hide your time capsule. Why did you choose that place?

3. Set up and label a display of your time capsule. Either collect the objects and put them in a box or draw pictures of the objects and display them on the bulletin board.

4. Invite people to look at your time capsule and explain why you chose each object.

Definition: A *time capsule* contains a collection of objects that tell people in the future about a particular place and time.

© 2005 *Talking, Writing and Thinking About Books* by Jo Phenix. Permission to copy for classroom use. Pembroke Publishers.

Adoption Posters

Imagine the animals in the story want to find homes with families.

1. Plan posters for 2 of the animals. Include

   - a description of appearance and behavior
   - reasons why the animal would make a good member of a family

Animal 1	Animal 2

2. Make posters. Include a picture of each animal.

3. Display your posters.

© 2005 *Talking, Writing and Thinking About Books* by Jo Phenix. Permission to copy for classroom use. Pembroke Publishers.

Descriptive Language

1. Choose a part of the story with good descriptive language. List the adjectives the author has used.

2. Choose a scene you know well and would like to describe. List adjectives you could you use in your description.

3. Use words from your two lists to write your description. Add an illustration.

© 2005 *Talking, Writing and Thinking About Books* by Jo Phenix. Permission to copy for classroom use. Pembroke Publishers.

Dictionary

Imagine you are writing a dictionary of words special to this story

1. Choose 10 words to use.

2. Print the words in alphabetical order. Beside each word, explain why it is important in this story.

Word	Importance in Story
_____	
_____	
_____	
_____	
_____	
_____	
_____	
_____	

© 2005 *Talking, Writing and Thinking About Books* by Jo Phenix. Permission to copy for classroom use. Pembroke Publishers.

Glossary

1. Choose 5 to 10 technical words from the story. Choose ones that everyone might not understand.

2. List the words in alphabetical order. Explain the meaning of each word.

Word	Meaning

Definition: A *glossary* is a special kind of mini-dictionary that explains the technical words in a story that readers may not understand.
Think: Will your glossary use illustrations?

© 2005 *Talking, Writing and Thinking About Books* by Jo Phenix. Permission to copy for classroom use. Pembroke Publishers.

Thesaurus

1. Choose about 10 words from the story.

2. List your words in alphabetical order. Beside each one, list as many alternate words as you can. When you have written as many as you can think of, do some research to find more.

Word	Alternatives

Definition: A *thesaurus* gives alternate words you can use. For example, instead of *hot* you might use *warm, fiery, roasting, scalding, blazing, sweltering, scorching.*
Hint: You will find more alternatives for adjectives and adverbs than for other types of words.

© 2005 *Talking, Writing and Thinking About Books* by Jo Phenix. Permission to copy for classroom use. Pembroke Publishers.

Word Collage

1. Make a list of words from the story. They could be

   • names of people and places
   • strong verbs
   • feelings and emotions
   • good adjectives

   or any other words you find interesting.

2. Check the spelling of all your words.

3. Print your words in interesting styles, colors, and sizes. Choose different kinds of paper to print your words on.

4. Paste your words on a large piece of paper to make a design.

> A *word collage* is a picture or design made up of words pasted on paper.

© 2005 *Talking, Writing and Thinking About Books* by Jo Phenix. Permission to copy for classroom use. Pembroke Publishers.

Alphabet Book

Example of the first page of an alphabet book:

Adrian ate an apple after arguing with Amy.

Use this model to write an alphabet book.

1. Using ideas from the story, write one sentence for each letter. Use that letter to start as many words in the sentence as possible.

A:	B:
C:	D:
E:	F:
G:	H:
I:	J:
K:	L:
M:	N:
O:	P:
Q:	R:
S:	T:
U:	V:
W:	X:
Y:	Z:

2. Fold and staple paper to make a book. Put one sentence on each page.

3. Illustrate your alphabet book.

Were there any letters you couldn't use?

© 2005 *Talking, Writing and Thinking About Books* by Jo Phenix. Permission to copy for classroom use. Pembroke Publishers.

5 Research

These activities will take the children outside the story, and outside the classroom into the school or public library. Some children may wish to do their search on the Internet; the search itself will contribute to the students' learning.

The activities will help raise awareness about an author, and may promote further reading of that author's work. Looking for books of the same type will help children develop a sense of genre, and help them pursue and widen their individual tastes.

The activities may also be useful in extending the children's non-fiction reading, as you use them in other subject areas, such as history or science.

Author Study • *Did You Know?* Poster • Book Display

Author Study

1. Find the name of the author of your story.

Author: _____

2. Find other stories or books by this author and write down the titles. Put a star beside those that are available in your school library.

3. Write 3 reasons why you would choose another story by this author.

Reason 1: _____

_____

Reason 2: _____

_____

Reason 3: _____

_____

4. Print your list and your reasons on a separate sheet.

5. Display your list for others to read.

© 2005 *Talking, Writing and Thinking About Books* by Jo Phenix. Permission to copy for classroom use. Pembroke Publishers.

Did You Know? Poster

1. Find out what country the story is set in.

Country: _____

2. Find a map of that country.

3. Find out 3 facts about the country that you did not know before.

Fact 1: _____

_____

_____

Fact 2: _____

_____

_____

Fact 3: _____

_____

_____

4. Make a *Did You Know?* poster to display what you have discovered.

© 2005 *Talking, Writing and Thinking About Books* by Jo Phenix. Permission to copy for classroom use. Pembroke Publishers.

Book Display

1. Set up a display to go with your story. Here are some ideas to get you started:

   • Books by the same author

   • Books about the same topic

   • Books set in the same place

   • Books of the same type; for example, mystery, adventure, humor.

2. Make an inviting sign to advertise your display.

© 2005 *Talking, Writing and Thinking About Books* by Jo Phenix. Permission to copy for classroom use. Pembroke Publishers.

Appendix: Activity Assessment

The activities in this book will not elicit the same response from each child. What we understand and how we respond are based on prior knowledge and experience, and often on age, personality, individual tastes, and personal and family values.

One purpose of this kind of response activity is for students to try out ideas and test hypotheses in a low-risk situation. Many of the responses will be in the form of first-draft writing. It is important to reinforce for students that the focus at this stage of the writing is on ideas and content, rather than on spelling accuracy and neatness. What we evaluate and respond to will indicate for our students what we think is most important. There will be many opportunities for the writing to be revised and edited, and for a final draft to be made, and at this time you can assess final-draft skills.

In the absence of right and wrong answers, assessment may be based on the quality of the student's involvement in the activity. Did the student understand and complete the task? Did the student contribute to group work? Can the student adequately justify choices and decisions?

An assessment master is provided for you to use on page 118. It is intended to supplement any regular, more detailed assessment you already do. You can use the master as a quick record of a student's work habits, engagement with the task, and quality of work. It is not necessary to use this master for every activity completed. Using it from time to time will highlight for you those students who are able to work effectively from the activities. If some students do not achieve well, you can monitor them more closely and more often.

There is also an assessment master for students to use (see Self-Assessment on page 119) to help them reflect on their work. Using this checklist may help them ensure that they are following instructions carefully and completing the tasks effectively. You can decide how often students complete the assessment master.

Assessment Master

Date	Name	√	Comments
Work habits	• Reads and follows instructions • Works cooperatively when required • Provides leadership in groups • Organizes self and work		
Quality of work	• Overall impression • Stays on topic • Shows originality of ideas • Completes tasks • Demonstrates learning		

Date	Name	√	Comments
Work habits	• Reads and follows instructions • Works cooperatively when required • Provides leadership in groups • Organizes self and work		
Quality of work	• Overall impression • Stays on topic • Shows originality of ideas • Completes tasks • Demonstrates learning		

Date	Name	√	Comments
Work habits	• Reads and follows instructions • Works cooperatively when required • Provides leadership in groups • Organizes self and work		
Quality of work	• Overall impression • Stays on topic • Shows originality of ideas • Completes tasks • Demonstrates learning		

© 2005 *Talking, Writing and Thinking About Books* by Jo Phenix. Permission to copy for classroom use. Pembroke Publishers.

Self-Assessment

Date	Activity	Yes or No	Comments
Work habits	I read the instructions carefully I organized my time well I organized my materials well		
Quality of work	I finished all parts of the job I used good ideas My presentations were interesting I feel good about my work		

What could have made my work better:

Date	Activity	Yes or No	Comments
Work habits	I read the instructions carefully I organized my time well I organized my materials well		
Quality of work	I finished all parts of the job I used good ideas My presentations were interesting I feel good about my work		

What could have made my work better:

© 2005 *Talking, Writing and Thinking About Books* by Jo Phenix. Permission to copy for classroom use. Pembroke Publishers.

Index of Activities

adding to the story, 71
adoption poster, 106
advertisement
   House for Sale, 77
   radio, 13
advice, 72
alien report, 93
alphabet book, 112
animation, 59
argument, 23
audience, 14, 15, 17, 19, 22, 26, 27,
   29, 31, 32, 33, 34
author
   letter, 102
   study, 114
awards ceremony, 28

biography, 83
blurb, 55
board game, 58
book
   alphabet, 112
   cover, 56
   display, 116
   jacket, 55
   poster, 54
   review, 95
   talk, 16
brochure
   travel, 79
bumper sticker, 94

CD cover, 53
chalk talk, 19
chapter, 81, 83, 97
character
   description, 62
   diary, 66
   new, 101

   speech, 21
coat of arms, 38
collage, 111
comic strip, 51
comparing and contrasting, 91
contents, 92
conversation
   reunion, 80
   telephone, 25
costume design, 42
cover
   book, 56
   CD, 53

description
   character, 62
   setting, 76
descriptive language, 107
design
   costume, 42
   hat, 37
   room, 45
   T-shirt, 41
dialogue, 33
diary
   character, 66
   your, 103
dictionary, 108
Did You Know? poster, 115
disagreement, 24
display, 38, 39, 40, 41, 42, 43, 47, 48,
   53, 54, 56, 59, 77, 79, 92, 94, 95,
   105, 106, 114, 115, 116

e-mail friend, 64
editorial, 80
emotions, 18

fact or fantasy, 96

friendly letter, 67
front page, 87

genre, 116
gift list, 70
giving advice, 72
glossary, 109
gossip, 26
greeting card, 36

hall-of-fame portrait, 43
hat design, 37
headlines, 82, 87, 104
House for Sale advertisement, 71

job
    interview, 68
    letter, 73

landscape painting, 47
letter
    author, 102
    friendly, 67
    job, 73
list
    gift, 70
    rules, 92

mapmaking, 44
masks, 29
memoir, 81
mime, 30
mobile, 60
model making, 46
movie title, 89
mural, 48

new character, 101
newspaper
    editorial, 80
    front page, 87
    headlines, 82
    story, 82, 87
news script, 22

oral reading, 17
overhead script, 52

paper-bag puppets, 32
paragraphs, 76, 80, 81
party plan, 104

paste up, 82, 87
picture postcard, 78
play reading, 33
poem
    word-list, 63
portrait
    hall-of-fame, 43
postcard, 78
poster
    adoption, 106
    book, 54
    country *Did You Know?*, 115
    rules, 100
    Wanted, 39
problem solving, 99
puppet
    paper-bag, 32
    show, 34

questions
    quiz, 84
quiz
    questions, 84
    Who Am I?, 74

radio advertisement, 13
recording, 13, 16, 27
report
    alien, 93
    school, 69
research
    author, 114, 116
    genre, 116
    setting, 115, 116
reunion conversation, 86
review, 95
room design, 45
rules
    list, 92
    poster, 100

scenes, 31, 50, 51
school report, 69
scrapbook, 57
script
    news, 22
    overhead, 52
    talk-show, 27
sequel, 98
setting
    description, 76

research, 115, 116
show and tell, 14
signs, 37, 43, 116
singing, 15
songwriting, 15
speech, 21, 28
    giving, 12
    in character, 21
    writing, 12
sticky notes, 65
story
    adding to, 71
    newspaper, 82, 87
    staircase, 85
    summary, 88
storyboard, 50
storytelling, 44, 46, 48, 49, 51, 52, 88
summary, 88

T-shirt design, 41
table of contents, 97

tableau, 31
talk
    book, 16
    chalk, 19
    show-and-tell, 14
talk-show script, 27
telephone conversation, 25
thesaurus, 109
time capsule, 105
timeline, 49
title, 15, 31, 50, 56, 87, 89, 90
totem pole, 40
travel brochure, 79
TV guide, 90

Wanted poster, 39
web site, 75
Who Am I? quiz, 74
word collage, 111
word-list poem, 63

your diary, 103